Seeking Sunsets and Vistas
Travels in Americana Landscapes

INTRODUCTION

I remember when I was a kid growing up in England, a school teacher asked me what I wanted to do with my life. Obviously, she laughed at my answer (to travel) because I also remember her shaking her head and telling me, 'That's not really a proper job.' Well, I've been travelling the world for a while now, and at this point it seems pretty good so far. Maybe she was hoping that I'd say something more regimented.

The fact is: Our paths are all uniquely different. If, like me, you choose a path less travelled, that's absolutely fine. The world has enough conformists. The world needs more people who explore and create. If you don't fit in, celebrate that, then get ready to show off your uniqueness. Our society has some rigid boundaries for people, and when you decide that you don't want to follow same path as everyone else, don't get discouraged. The best way to find your trail in life is to start with a dream and then seek others who will aid you in your journey.

My love for the outdoors has helped me walk the path that I knew I needed to be on. I'm consciously aware of trying to cultivate my body and mind. When you're sensitive, it means you're aware of everything that's happening around you - details in the world that sometimes others miss. I've been exploring the world since I was a teenager, when I first felt the connection to the countryside. I've always found something soothing and truthful in its trails. When you're trying to expand your mind and fitness, travel and exercise are key.

Matt Hayden

BROTHERHOOD OF WANDERERS

We are all connected,
All on a journey, me and you,
Searching the trails in nature's tapestry
No matter what route we do.
And each memory has a part to play,
With heart and soul and wanderlust mind,
To seek vistas that offer fresh hope
When hope can be hard to find.

And though our routes may be different
The journey is the same inside,
We all need the distraction of nature
To offer comfort and guide.
Our paths are often interwoven,
And troubles can be abound,
Reach out to the fresh breaths of nature,
The brotherhood of the vagabond.

MOUNTAIN STAR

Mountain Star
Lights the way
For memories that change
Like night to day -
And bless the journey
That snakes through time
No matter the route -
Shines the way.

MAN IN THE WOODS

This man is not all he seems:
His roots lost in days long ago,
In bootleg times of yesterday;
And through his mind at sunset blow
The echoes of bygone dreams.

Though memories his mind does mill
Are all his lifestyle holds now,
And though he does not even know
What yields his fathers used to plough,
The bootlegger is a bootlegger still.

Beneath his wary weather-eye
And tired, unhurried woodland tread,
The townsfolk may easily ignore,
Yet all the buried stories ahead
With Americana greet his passing by.

METH-HEAD

Images motionless were seen to move
Outwards; the streets crawled
Down steep night time sidewalks to where
The riverside bars sprawled:

Dark promises of shadow life flowed
With the meth-head toiling;
Drenched heavily in summer heat,
The limbs of life boiling:

And, he veers aside, the body's flagging will
Hung in one moment, poised under the Kentucky hill.

FOREST TEMPLE

I too lay in such a temple:
Tall columns with the heavenly airs
Flowing between.
But my spirit, that had been gripped with pain
Tense and quivering,
Suddenly loosened, hovered a moment,
Swerved, slow-drifting
Through the columns of pine into clear night:
Floated in still ecstasy
Over age-old humanity, but for winged freedom
Incorrigible,
Impotent before it's old gods.

KENTUCKY MOONSHINERS

Crooks strive
In the night.
Police prejudice
In the night.
Kentucky Moonshiners fight
In the night.

LAKESIDE HOPE

Give me the wonders of wilderness and hope,
The sound of mountain breeze at night,
The wild whispers of lakeside waves
In the magic of the fresh dawn light.
Souls as fragile as the ebbing tide,
Drifting and dowsing the sandy bay,
I fight the stirring emotions of living,
Dreaming of sailing far away.

I've worked and travelled the land,
Ventured to wilderness very far,
But I still yearn a place to rest
Where the lakeside sprites are.
Give me a trail, a journey to discover,
The waiting time I feel is over,
The wilds want my heart to hold fast,
Spirits follow my footsteps in clover.

NEW MEXICO COYOTES

When fireflies begin to flicker
Over the meadows near the hills,
Ghosts-of-the-mountains,
The coyotes, stride into dusk

Over the meadows, a pack of ghosts,
Over the stubbled knolls,
Whispering barks,
The sound of hunt unfurling,
In the soft hue of starlight
To stalk the wasteland here.

Before the shapes of mist
Scattering foe beneath the moon,
Across field and trails the shrieks
Will know the claws of fire,
Swift devils stalking out of space.

WILD POETRY

Sweet wild spirit that sings in wanderlust days
Within the forest-foliage of my mind
I come with eager feet by devious ways
My unbound soul and joyous heart to bind.

I would encage thoughts in a verse of gold
But there's no cage, however strong, to please me;
The wilds come, sweet spirit, the wind grows cold,
Oblivion with it's icy breath will freeze thee.

Teach my wild heart to nestle in my soul
Before the frost of life takes it's toll.

DUSK #1

Never seen nor heard by most,
The creatures, souls, spirits of fauna,
Seldom seen by day,
Make haste and go about nocturnal ways,
In their stealthy night time stray,
Down tracks and trails,
Collecting discarded day-time scraps,
Eager for carefree play.

CHARLIE'S BAR

The happy sound is banter
And by all us is felt,
It ushers in understanding,
And can wash away all hesitation.
We all share joys of our lives,
And somehow deep inside
We miss those days of happiness,
Which somewhere must have died.

The summers of our childhood,
Seemed so long and bright and warm,
But now as time is passing by
They seem to darken down.
The joys of exploration pass us,
And with each year we now begin,
To look at life in different ways
A strange fear has settled in.

THE GHOST OF SANDIA CREST

My friend said
That ghosts had their homes beneath
The rocky mounds of Sandia Crest.
He pointed to a snow topped knoll
And indicated there below
A cave. He poked his waking stick
Into the twisted grass,
Towards the trails and pass,
'That's where
The old ghosts live,' he said
'Up there in the mountains.'

He never knew
That I, just a vagabond,
Had heard and understood
The tales of Americana ghosts.
Imaging the realms of New Mexico
I clasped his shoulder in timid knowing
And long retained an awed belief
In the hidden world of Sandia Crest.

STACY THE STRIPPER

There's no deception in her air,
In every word she does make bare
A heartfelt soul.
Her eyes do sparkle, her love is pure,
But life can be hard as sure,
On the stripper's pole.

THE MICHIGAN VETERAN

Desolate that cry as though life were unwanted
See now, rounding the street, a forlorn veteran,
Trembling worn hands grasping the evening air,
Weary and ghostly, careless of the scattering grime.

This is the alley dweller that stumbles like a clown,
Buffeted by dreams, almost extinct, who has chosen,
So fragile a man, to live on furious streets.

Here where winds whistle in funnels, and chill the backs
Of bustling locals and valiant tourists,
In bellowing shadows that shelter the workmen
The Michigan veteran wavers along the sidewalk.

WAKING IN RICHMOND

How good it is, to wake and hear
The dawning breeze from far and near,
The Atlantic that teases across shall lure
The rolling waves upon the shore.
Through dunes the hiker without a care,
Sends salty scents in chill morning air.
Sweet sing the gulls in nearby tree
Heralding a Carolina dawn for me.

City sounds it seems, are hardly heard,
No traffic sounds, nor yet a faulting word.
Though seeds will now begin to sow,
And all this beauty starts to go.
But in my dreams I shed no tear,
For each dawn I wake I know I'll hear,
Sweet songs of tussled sea
Heralding a Carolina dawn for me.

MID-EAST STATE

The homes, and town, and towers of grain,
The woods, and streams, and hills, and plains
Her stories and gems.
Her treasures are laid out on high,
And the good spirits in the sky
It's dearest friends.

THOUGHTS OF LUST

Walking through the town,
Distracted by the pain,
Disillusioned for the moment
The wilderness thought gone again.

A mind once full of lust,
Of future and consent,
Now seems so quiet and empty
And no longer quite content.

But the mist will slowly stray,
Here eyes will sparkle clear,
And once again with mind now buoyed,
Fresh thoughts will re-appear.

Unleashed thoughts can now begin,
And mirror once again,
With clarity she and I understand
All erotic plans that stem.

THE SUMMIT SUN

Sat on the mountain summit, to watch
The end of day now unfold,
Nature's palette across wild skies
In hues of reds and gold,
Reflected in the tranquil creek,
Whose soft, clear waters,
Hide secrets and stories
Of the Americana falters;
The land of lore, as old as time
With Man's footsteps in tow,
The surging power of the land,
With mountain peaks aglow.
This magic hour of early dusk
Mixed with Atlantic sea air,
Blends with the departing sun
For wanderlust fools to share.

DAWN MIST IN PHONIEX

Dawns another day.
Round the derelict church
Cold mist curls
Shroud-formed and grey.

We two sit safe
Warm wrapped in moving
Drifts of blanket wool.
No sound disturbs this rest
Save the eternal traffic
Over the distant crest.

THE FORESTS DARK

Scary visions and frightening sounds
In my mind still I try to avoid.
Heading through this darkness
I can't really sense my movements,
Seems to be darkness all abound.
Nothing here, to light up my journey
And footsteps snaking to where I'll end.
Won't even count the stride these days,
I'm fooled by myself,
Lost in the wilderness haze.

THE WANDERERS

Some seem born to wander, homeless,
To stretch their souls and seek no rest
The constant learning of the other,
The journey a never-ending test.

DUSK #2

While up above this summer trail,
Sits hunched within the darkened tree,
The Red-Kite of prey,
Who with hawkish swoop.
Alights upon the fragile down below,
It stalks
Then flies off to some hidden lair,
To hunt and feed it's needy young,
So that with the coming of dusk,
With souls and stomachs full,
We once again can sleep till another day.

THE WANDERERS AT DAWN

The eager band of wanderers,
On winding trail to wend,
In shrouds of spring sunshine,
Into the wilderness transcend.

Wild Kentucky delights the eye,
Of every outdoors folk fair,
The winding creeks, hills of spruce,
Secret sanctuaries that offer prayer.

To saunter on the mountainside,
Gipsy living, the wild spell to yield,
Light mist descending from distant peaks,
Adds to the dreamlike appeal.

Burdens light, of banters lends,
This wild carefree living,
A rendezvous of easy hours,
Beside nature's giving.

A CABIN IN NORTH KENTUCKY

A backwoods cabin in disarray,
With paint all peeled and roof astray,
It's porch - broken & spent,
With creaking boards that bow and sway,
A chimney stack that's bent.

In moonshine days there was a still,
Until the Feds took a swill,
It's iron lie in the dirt,
The boiler dump is still on there hill,
Lost in memories of hurt.

Idyllic bliss or desolate squat,
Where families once dreamed,
Now lost, like the Americana.
A homestead now gleaned
For dust and fauna.

SUNSET IN SKI TOWN

The day is charged with sunset's hallowing,
Grave orange hues bathe half the horizon's rim
Remote and steep and far the sky recedes
Blue- green and airy, dreaming of distant sea.
The slim pine-trunks grow ruddy in the glow
And mountains burn with a pinkish fire,
Take on a larger dignity, and shed
The common day's familiarity;
Subdued, the skier chants his evensong,
And silence, which is day's last benison
Falls on the slopes and the nestling town.

THE BACKWARDS BUDDHA

        Scarcely do I notice him
        Lost in futile wandering,
        Tatty clothes on a shadow,
    Whatever character he can muster
Hard won from memories and seething rain,
The febrile convergence of nature, the unseen
Unrest of realms and worlds, the wind-
        Begotten whispers of the lost, the lonely
        Spirits perishing in the dark.

AMONG MOUNTAINS

How I love hiking in the mountains;
Carefree fondled by country breeze,
Moments and memories pierce the sky
Amidst the sea of forest trees.
I recall a towering white peak
Where wanderers climbed to sit
And find what Shamans seek,
Souls lost in drifting cloud,
Stories stored by the proud.
I have wandered in the mountains,
Through times of gladden talk
And with springtime long gone,
I recall the journeys made,
And favour the mountains - every one.

THE COYOTE IN EUREKA HILLS

This journey I heard
The coyote call
Over the southern hills.
The red sun rested
In the western sky.
The trickster of my dreams
Around me cried.
Every trail and every road
Held stories with heavy load,
Heart breaking, joy rising
To journey in evening strides.

Let come dreams what may
Here at the ending of the day
When solitary ghosts
Homeward fly
And lengthening shadows
In the desert lands lie,
What matter anything at all
Except
I heard the coyote call.

THE FLEETING SUMTER SPRITE

Fleeting is the sprite's visit,
Touching light the loner's rich lust,
Experience the unseen treasure,
Life's lesson - in the self to trust.

KATIE

The beauty of the Vermont dawns,
The big sky light is thine;
Yet all my dreams of lustful nights
Dwell within her blue eyes shine.
Not statelier in her darkness
The nimble limbs grandly move,
And in her smile is youth and joy,
And in her voice is playful love.

SOOTHING SOLITUDE DREAMS

O gentle earth, mother of me: O mountains
That know no fear, I kneel to you,
I seek you with wistful tears and cry
That you will turn your tender heart to mine
As mothers to their crying young turn.
Touch me, and soothe away those flogging fears
Those nightmares making havoc of the night,
And whisper to me low that perfect dream,
That lovely secret that is peace to know,
That touch the silence tells you in the dark.

THE PENNSYLVANIA TINKER

As I wandered, I was aware
There grew before my tired eyes
A little tinker too bright and fair,
Too strangely captivating for surprise.
She held the beauty of the place
Had suddenly become concrete,
So full of nature's grace,
From her wide eyes and flushed face
Down to her little dirt-caked feet.
Her clothes were tainted and old
Twined with fancy fold on fold,
That gave no hint where, nestled well,
What dainty joys might warmly dwell,-
A tinker of majestic grace was she,
So quaint, so lost, so fragile, she was,
The mirror image of me.

DUSK #3

The darkness brings dreams,
Moving in their quiet ways
The 'Gateway to Realms' I do suppose,
Their destinations reincarnate,
Whipped by changes we cannot see,
And only awareness touches the earth,
And buffet at our frailty.
For only then,
Can wanderers perceive their worth.

RECOLLECTIONS

I wandered through the deep Americana woods
On trails that poets of past had tread,
And I recall those warm, early summer days
With moments and memories in my head.
I pictured the crystal-clear creeks hidden,
Sometimes feeling the carefree air there,
Or the warm skinny-dip mountain lake
That promised blissful favours everywhere.

I wander the ice-cool mountain stream,
The life-enriching waters cool.
And watch the carefree eagles high above,
The blue herons by the silent pool.
Happy journeys I do recollect,
The shamanic lessons that were fed,
And so I drift to the past realms
With new travels to take in my head.

THE OWL

Dry leaves swirl
Ahead of footsteps
Along the night-still forest path
Beside the stream;
While overhead
The lone stoic owl
Has left her daytime bed,
And chill winds spoil
The memory of old hunts.

FOREST SPRITES OF VERMONT

Should you hike in forests of pine
On some deserted trail, you may find
That you can the faintest of sound
Of sprightly whispers all around.
Those tinker sprites enjoy the tease
With songs of mischief on the breeze.

THE VAGABONDS

So stoic, so bold, the vagabonds,
Who pay no heed to nature's chills,
But stride defiant, sharp and bright
To fill bleak souls with hope and light,
And seek the hearts of all who glance
Upon their wild and wanderlust stance,
Their minds buoyed in gallant stout
To find the last of the wilds out.
Such happiness their journeys mean,
While heralding the new vistas seen.

FIRST DAY IN MAINE

From high vista I feast my eyes
On hills and mountains softly dressed
With green and yellows of autumn's guise,
Stark, majestic, motionless.

Except for mists and clouds so dark
Blowing, drifting overhead
As if they wanted to embark
From ocean far they fled.

A damp morning, first for me
North so far - such wilderness
In this wild land of poetry
Inspired by its own mood expressed.

Dramatic changes - shifts of breeze
Sunlight, shadows, fog and rain.
Its rage and temper unbound
As if for me to entertain.

I'm stoic in wanting to roam
Out yonder exploring as I please.
But the guesthouse will be home;
This day beckons rest and ease.

Perhaps a new dawn will bring sun,
A chance to stride northwards fresh
The scenes and views today I shun,
That from the doorway I assess.

LONESOME WOODS

I too have hiked
In lonesome woods
Along old paths
By crystal streams,
And heard the songbirds
In rhyme
Where sun-shafts through
The pine gleam -
Shuffle the earth
Underfoot,
And share the forest stories
As you go -
I too have hiked
In lonesome woods
And watched the life
Of stories grow.

MOUNTAIN STORMS

The wind, clean mad, bawls in across the deep;
Crouching in valleys, quiet; leaping out
With sudden howls and treacherous gusts, to flout
Unwary feet. Within, the wild dreams leap;
The beaten yellow mountain tents defy
Stoutly the loud bombardment of the rain;
And in the midst of the fierce hurricane
Peril and glory pass their shelter by.

THE SPIRIT OF VAGABONDS

I am the song the vagabond sing;
The journey of the realms.
I am the lone bee willing to sting;
The wind blowing through elms.

I am the eagle in the sky;
Drifting effortless like a cloud.
The lone wolf stalking sly;
I am the white bear, stoic and proud.

I am the stories, dark and old;
The drifters coming in from sea.
I am the tale Guthrie told
The crude carving on the tree.

I am the wanderlust hiking alone;
The gentle mountainside stream.
I am the vistas that folks have known
And the realities of the ancient dream.

GREENBRIEAR STATE FOREST

The way was hard from the trailhead,
Marauding saplings and ripe blueberries
Stifled paths among forgotten giant.
And cabins half-forgotten, where broken
        dreams
Rotted in sundry valleys chosen
With special care not so long ago.

SPOKANE RAIN

Through the summer week
The rain falls on the leaves
And the forest trees
Sway and tussle
To and fro, to and fro.

This sweet recollection
Weaves
Into my daydreams
And seems to tell
Some vagabond story
Wise and sweet withal,
One which I cannot
Now fathom or find,
Which lies, fleeting.
Buried wisdom
In the debris of my mind.

NIGHTMARES IN SOLITUDE

I slept, and dreamed of darkness,
Solitude and lightning flashes.
I walked in storm-tossed forests
Beaten by night's muddled lashes.

I strolled through mudded glades,
Hidden by the blackest night;
Fearful I slunk in terror
In search of light, daytime light.

WILD TRAILS

They disappear where no one
Ever went but drifters and you
Looking for something
Else or for nothing
But some wild beyond
Wilds that you knew.

Sudden in old valleys
You found them buried
Alive in shadow
But awaiting somehow
In the shades stray warmth
Where they chose to be.

Where the wanderers go
In search of nothing
But what might be there
Till the dusks draw in
Beyond the wilds
They know you know.

BIG RIDGE STATE PARK

The trees would be heavy
With sparkling dew,
Each pine in the forest
Wafted perfume.
But nights were cold
Now that summer was past.
I would be glad
To be warm at last.
I hiked today
To the Kentucky border.
I'll stay here alone
In this ancient land,
Be inspired to write
Better thoughts - the plan.

DON'T BE LONELY

Away with loneliness, my jilted people
Come walk with me, stride forward, not back,
For a new journey has begun for us.
Now we must seek, my drifters. For so long
Life for us stood still; now we know
Times are changing, life is progress,
Life is journeying out; life is onward.
Wise men had to learn wanderlust ways,
Now it is our turn.
Away with staleness and the urban past;
Let us try to understand the wildness ways
And accept nature as nature accepts us;
Let us judge wise people by their best.

THE WILDS OF KENTUCKY

I seek the wilds of Kentucky countryside.
When glorious Spring's own treasures hide
Among the forest hills and shaded dales;
A river snakes by a mossy stone,
Or bears which hunt alone,
And birds amid the tuneful vales.

I seek the wilds of Kentucky countryside,
When Summer spreads its offerings wide,
In valleys or on mountain heights,
And tries to make my thoughtless earth
Then realise fond Americana worth
By long displays of nature's sights.

I seek the wilds of Kentucky countryside,
When Autumn finds itself denied
Creation of the land's delights,
Prepares the State for Winter's cold,
And turns the hills from green to gold,
While whispering of the coming blights.

I seek the wilds of Kentucky countryside,
When blanched by Winter's snowy tide,
Short days which long nights help disperse -
And so the seasons of Americana come and go
In sunshine, rainy Fall, or in snow,
And Americana rules the wild verse.

OLD TRAILS WEST

The trail sweeps out west,
Straight into the sun's unblinking gaze,
And I know the journey is ancient;
That the world is wild,
That it sometimes speaks directly to us
With the voice it chooses,
And with untethered actions.

THE MIDNIGHT BATHE

Tears stripped him naked to the night,
Wave on grey wave the tide came in;
He waded out breast high and swam
Among the star wakes shimmering tin.
The pebbles dragged along the shore
With dismal dreams in his ear;
The strong swell pulled - and then he knew
All in a moment deadly fear:
This tide was Death, whose hungry love
With wave and swell was drawing him
Against his stubborn weary will
With feverish urgency to sea.

THE AMERICANA WORLD

I've seen the Americana world,
Each separate State known,
And realised that none excelled
On their own;
I've longed for America's well known capes
And bays,
And yearned to gaze again upon her hills
Incised with valleys full of sparkling rills
Which turn to dreams
During lost summer days.

THE TENNESSEE TINKER

She gently soothed my cautious mind,
And bade it to be calm;
For soulful scars of every kind,
She knew a healing balm.

In times of anxiety or of pain,
When I was lost alone,
She showed me how to live and reign
In realms of my own.

Often she was present near me.
During night and day,
Always she was there to cheer me,
When anxious dreams crossed my way.

And once when darkness held my soul -
She deigned her name to tell,
Then claimed allegiance as her toll,
Before she said farewell.

Some folks called her The Tennessee Tinker,
But few can know her worth,
Yet, she is the guide to realms for me
While dreams are lost on Earth.

FOURTH OF JULY

Where are the spirits that built
America's fame?
Are they souls buried in the past?
Who shall take their place, and share
Their name
Remembered by the country till the last?

THE SAN JOSE LOVER

Man and waitress seek the pleasure
They will muster in equal measure
And the joy will generously spread
With greatest pleasure in their explicit bed
And they will enjoy the hazy night
With exquisite abandon and sheer delight
In the motel bed they do embrace
Between their limbs there is little space
With each other they take the delight
They are seeking each their favourite
Let no one dare judge their bliss
Whilst they indulge in each sinful kiss
The guilt can wait for morning sun
For it is pushed aside for lustful fun.

DRIFTING

Let me explore alone and roam at will
Among the forests of Kentucky yonder hill;
There let me drift along till tired I be,
Alone in wilds will my soul be free.

Let me drift - for longings of my heart
Tell me to wander by dawn's shining start.
The wilds shall join in my delight,
And share my joyous raptures day and night.

Let me roam across Kentucky's sunny plains,
In those old towns, along those quiet lanes.
There I can roam without a single care -
For nought with Americana can compare.

SUNSET BELOW EL MALAPIS

The darting birds sing
Their evening song.
Long,
Lie the shadows
On the dusty worn trail.
The southern sun,
Burning red,
Lightly floating,
Heart of fire,
Commands the summer sky.

Blest the dirtbaggers three
Who now together run
Beneath the ancient El Malpais hill.
Blessed indeed to see,
To meet, to greet,
The trickster coyote,
As brother
And as friend
Here in this solitary place
At the summers day end.

RIVER SWANS

Beneath the silver pall of night,
I could see them gliding past -
Let those lost swans take their flight,
Daylight soon shall see the last,

Effortless, carefree, floating shapes,
On the river gliding swift,
Night the banks with darkness drapes,
Soft and silent on they drift.

The imagination's charms
Welcomes dreamlike swans to appear:
Who could have but vague alarms -
Calmness proves the caution of fear.

How I long to see them now;
Dreams to see them yet once more -
I would watch them then and plough
My swift way to a ghost realm's shore.

THE LONELY ONE

Come lonely one, hike with me,
Across the hills to the sea.
To the land where the sun's for all,
Lay on dunes and hear seabirds call.

Forget the passing time of day,
In the cool ocean bays we'll play.
Seek out the sirens of ocean blue,
Singing songs of heartache just for you.

Come lonely one, hike in the land of free,
Shelter beneath the shadows of a tree.
Let nature fill your soul with fun,
Come hike with me, under summer sun.

TWILIGHT TRAIL

Where the wanderlust trail will take me
Through the sheltered, tree-lined lane;
On a journey on fresh discovery,
As the summer day starts to wane;
When the evening air cools us
Pushed by darkness of twilight breeze,
As it stirs thoughts of town living
Far from the maddening trails and trees;
It's a joy to recall the countryside met
As I journey down homeward way,
Taking in the last moments of vistas
To savour at the remnants of this day.

SUMMER NIGHT

Moon shines bright
Sky is clear
Breeze is warm
Explorers cheer

THE STEAMY FOREST

The forest steams this morning
Old trails damp
From night-time rain.
In each corner glade
Cold campsite drifters
Are drinking coffee
In the breathless quiet
Of solitude paths.

Soon the drifters will be joined
By embassies of fauna.
A vapid majesty
Will seep with joyous
Pomp and bustle.
The drifters will sweat
To keep the curios at bay.

THE ANCIENT MOUNTAIN

With a sagging heart I left, but still
In the new even life there is no rest:
The wild mountain has enthralled me;
And I come back beneath white driven sails
Running before the shattering gales
Until the stoic peeks above the sea
Brim clear. I dream and run
Towards the winding stairway to the sun
And as I climb my heart beats fast,
Where it will break at last.

HEADING INLAND

I tire now of the Atlantic beach,
Where blustery winds try to reach.
Follow the trailhead by the trees,
Head for hills with subtle ease.
We'll stride out into sacred land,
Shake off the residues of Atlantic sand.
I tire not of what lays ahead,
The coastal paths we'll no longer tread.

THE FLORIDA FLUNKY

It seems, at last, his wicked heart is cold
I heard his death bell has tolled.
Good it is that the evilness has fled
And happier is Florida that the flunky is dead.

His story is dark with warped desire
Smothered with torment and fire.
He stained all with obscene reign
A drifter masked a liar once again.

It is good that he does not see tomorrow
The Florida flunky who brought so much sorrow.
One last toll of his satanic bell
Led his soul into an earthly hell.

FLEETING SUMMER

Passing quick the midsummer haze,
Lasting but thirty nights and thirty days.
The short-lived blooms fed the seed,
By warm caress the poets feed.

LAST OF THE LONELY PLACES

Mourn for the last of the lonely places
Filled with the wanderlust tune
And the haunting cry of a lost bird
Under a drifting moon.

Weep for all the plundered vistas
And everything they ever meant
Of joy and beauty, peace, solitude
And life's needed replenishment.

Remember them, the last lonely places
Where once wild hearts beat.
Remember them for they lie fractured -
Beneath Man's foolish feet.

SPRINGTIME IN SARATOGA

Distant now it may seem,
Winter seeps just like a dream.
Trees awake, birds do sing.
The freshness of a Saratoga spring.

Hikers come each springtime day,
Wanderlust fools come out to play.
Climbers seek the mountain scent,
While poets sit with vistas content.

The warmer breeze and sways of green,
Dulled winter souls seek the scene.
This season, it's delights to bring
Our souls soar, for it is spring.

ARIZONA EMOTIONS

Melancholy is near, his dreams are calling,
A silent tear comes a-rolling.
The city wind blows the emotions around.
He quickens his steps to cover ground,
To seek the shelter of the warm indoors,
Hoping the emotions won't flout his flaws.
He'll talk up concepts of happier days,
Seeking warmth from where others lay,
Sleep in blankets through all night long,
Hoping to find a dream he can belong.

WALKING ON A WINDY DAY

My spirit is woken, my soul is soaring
And drifting carefree on the breeze;
For the wild winds around are roaring
Arousing the ghosts in the trees.

The withered fauna is huddled and hiding
In shadows of tall pines - stoic but sly,
Whilst hikers are warm and merrily striding
Through the weathers from the pewter sky.

Misty rains streaming through the trees,
The hikers seek the warm log den,
The harsh dampness of the breeze,
Seeking to persist till then.

GHOSTLY SOLACE

After the storms had passed,
The moon slowly rose,
Silvering the forest trees,
And underneath their
Snowy canopies,
The hikers lay,
Bright scattered tents
On the trails,
Wet from the rain under
Giant trees.
A ghost took flight from a Redwood,
Dreaming by moonlight, to pass
On his unfaltering way
Through the bright night,
And, scattered on the trail,
Like weary fauna,
Quiet the hikers lay.

DEAD POETS

The words of many mighty poets dead
Bear up my soul: I float on them,
As vistas lift the vagabond's head
And move about nature's requiem.
From ocean waters they and I
Float out to tryst of sea and sky.

THE LOVELY VIXEN

What emotions for my sensuous eyes,
The lovely vixen,
Liberal and lusty,
Sleek, hot and busty.
Seeking the material things in life,
She yearns for more.
Small-town living takes it's wants,
But it is not what she lives for.
She stalked the fields of my emotions,
She found my weakness and set in for kill.
Lunging for my heart, scarring me for life,
Draining me of seed and strife.
Too shameful to help herself,
Her soul always belonged to someone else.
Finding no way in,
We'll meet at the bitter end.

WANDERLUST HIKERS

The hikers go to and fro
In vagabond patrol,
Their only wish in life to go
Where vistas point the goal;
Or if for other ends they rove
It is to find a wanderlust love.

HAPPINESS

A sunny morning,
Running barefoot
Along dew-drenched trails
Picking vistas
To remember:
I was happy there.

GHOSTLY FLIRT

A deserted bar, the town quite still,
A dreamy kind of day;
I leaned upon the old bar,
My thoughts drifting miles away.
I guess because I was dreaming
And seemed soothed by the scene,
There appeared a girl of beauty,
Hair of gold, eyes of green.
A radiant siren, a dream I thought,
Oh, a classic sight for a guy to see,
And truly she presented everything
A smouldering lover that could be.
She sat on a stool not too far
So vivid in neon light,
He silky skin seemed to glow
Quite lustfully bright.
I watched enchanted, as if a spell,
And longed for her to stay
But as I turned around in my chair
The beauty left to go and stray.

SAN CARLOS RESERVATION

Full summer moon
Wonderful, joyous,
Floating cream white
Against the velvet
Of a desert night.

Gypsies wander entranced
Under grand ghostly moonlight,
Shamans seek visions
With each grand vista
And the unstable of mind
Find their wandering voices
Lost, moon-crossed.

Full summer moon
Silently drifting
Over the sleeping land:
Ever trying to teach us
Stories we cannot
Hear or understand.

CABIN FEVER

The sad dull eyes look outward from the trees,
The dusty nostrils quiver,
Grey lips and whitened eyes; they stare
Of those dead memories lost on breeze,
Scattered with anxious shiver,
The living grace. Was it for pride,
Was it for pity he fled out here,
To blazon how his soul died?

DREAMS OF FRIDAYS IN FORESTS

Mists tease the lake.
Still waters break,
Paddles slice against clear water -
The kayaks are drifting.

Camp fire
Fizzes off the damp.
Tired souls sleep in silence.
No one stirs.

I see them now, as dreams shake my sleep.
Rapt in them, I'm captured
In forms of my own dream
Of sleeping by the fire.

MIRROR IMAGE

I gaze into the eyes of my lusty vixen,
Her reflection as dark as my soul,
I see my emotions on her face,
Telling stories of vice and sin,
Reflections of a tattered past,
Dreams cast into the forgotten bin.
The story of a sacrificed love,
The objective was personal gain,
Sexual band-aids for hidden pain.
Lacking morals and angelic wisdom,
All we see are souls alone.
In our evolving and soiled world,
I see a woman who's morals are thinning,
With a stranger of dark sinning.
As the devil had intended,
The ghosts of lust are grinning.

UNDER THE OPEN SKY

Down here how calm the valley
And overhead
The white clouds one by one serenely pass
Far lovelier than a marijuana dream
Above the soft bed of summer grass.
The whisper of Americana is in my ears -
Better, I thought, than poisoned tears
And wanderlust muffled feet,
For I lie like a gently fallen ghost
Or a folded memory.
No room is here for foolish boast
Here where I come to write,
Since life was sweet, sweet be its day of death
Under open sky plight.

LOST VOICES

We are the lost souls who by no choice,
Sought to lose the optimistic voice,
The hippies, the lost drifters,
The vagabonds, the weary grifters,
Seeking the country bend,
Its purpose to a different end;
We hide in the shadows, welcome another day,
Dream of happier days slipped away.
Dirtbaggers out running the trail,
Enjoyment had without a fail.
Outsiders look into our playground and say
'Are they souls who've lost their way?'
But we're the Americana gatekeepers,
The wildness seekers.

EAGLES OF DEEP CREEK

The eagles stoop and disappear
Beneath the dusky span
Content to observe from year to year
The foolish haunts of man.
They half forget the old delight:
The woods where they should fare
In joy of tumultuous flight
Like tempests in plains of air.

NEW MEXICO MOUNTAINS

The scudding clouds
Raced across the sky
The wild wind blew
Unabatedly.

Grand mountains pink
Stood stoic and fine
Across the far
Horizon line.

Soul rinsed by
The cool evening breeze
Our dreams chased
The trails that tease.

LAKOTA HILLS

The dusk sun illuminated our way
Getting high on lust and grass
The wind blew out across the hills
And we stood aghast
The sanctuary of the lonesome place
Deserted, distant and wild
Brought sultry thoughts to mind
Fun of the wildness kind.

THE WOODLAND AT PELHAM FALLS

We saunter through the tumbled woods
Imagining jaunts around fire-lit camps,
Plucked memories and stories,
A close and living spirit,
An order of the realms:
Of consciousness.
Of lives always changing,
Of life, changing,
While silently, unseen tired spirits
Consume the fated journeys.

A WANDERLUST VISTA

Summer days and warm mornings
Lift vagabond hearts and minds,
Watching eagles serenely gliding
Where the Kentucky river winds,
Feeling gentle breezes blowing
As the puffy clouds drift by,
Hearing small birds in tree-tops
And the carefree larks on high.

And so the miles swiftly pass,
The trail soon slips away,
Whilst in the west a poets glow
Announces fading day.
And soon the sky is streaked,
And filled with reds and gold,
A perfect ending to a summer's day,
A wanderlust vista to behold.

TIMELESS JOURNEY

We walked through towns deep in Americana lore.
And hand in hand smiled in delighted glee,
For there was nature and townsfolk in harmony
And history filled our day with gaiety.

We sat dreaming, drowsy under summer heat,
As timeless hours drifted by with silent wings.
We bared our feet and cooled them in the stream
And laughed and loved and shared secret things.

As soaring eagles shared our well-loved trail,
Soft breezes swayed the giant trees,
We vowed we would one day come back again,
For this was a journey to continue as we please.

AMERICANA PEACE

Go seek the highway that runs out to sky,
Away from the blights of the city street.
Go find a vista where ocean winds sweep by,
And valley breezes wait to greet.

Go seek a peace where eagles swoop,
Haunting where the quiet waters gleam.
Go seek a riverbank where ancient trees stoop,
Over snaking crystal waters of a stream.

In the green wilderness, life is good.
The burdens of life ease, some cease.
For the serenity of the wild wood,
Brings a calmness of Americana peace.

THE TWIN LAKES LIGHT

In shrouds of green dappled bright
The wild forests trap the morning light.
And secret meadows nestle around,
Seeking out simply pleasures on sacred ground.
Such sanctuary settles the spirit whole,
Brings comfort to a scatty soul,
And warms, when even days are grey,
Promises of spring never far away.
And the wanderlust can once again return
To vistas for which our souls yearn,
And feel eased emotions laid bare,
To savour the country, sunlit air,
While wild birds softly sing
And outdoor folk welcome the return of spring.

WHEN WANDERLUST CALLS

Only as in the dark he lies awake,
Hearing the cry of his city captivity,
And cannot speak of dreams in his days,
Nor ease his bonds; he ventures for his sake
Beyond shallow walls, unreasoningly,
And wading into unknown wilds, he prays.

DEEP CREEK DAYDREAMS

On warm spring days, how sweet
To step beyond the binding city street,
And seek wanderlust where dreams lie
Hidden amongst country under Eastern sky;
Where waterfalls and lost creeks pour
And snow-peaked mountains soar -
No tears, no fears, a sanctuary apart
To ease the urban soul and weary heart.

And, when the hikers all are gone,
For country folk life still goes on,
And follows, through springtime days,
Americana of time-honoured ways;
Of rustic living, through smiles and tears,
Sustained by wanderlust through the years,
Each fresh season brings vagabond thrills,
Nestled under shadows of Americana hills.

SPRING IN CHERRY SPRINGS STATE PARK

The weather is warm, down in the sheltered lane,
Where few wanderers pass. A shelving, stony bank,
Topped by a lonely copse, holds at bay the wind -
The rough, winter's end wind, fresh from snowy
                Hills.
Under the bank, the sapling blueberry bushes nestle,
Their fruity gifts waiting for the all-day light.
Dormant trees eagerly wait for blossom. Song birds dart
Among the fragile grass and secluded mammals forage,
And on cold currents, eagles up high flit and flirt,
Mingled chorus of intent fill the spring air.
Suddenly, seclusion falls. The clouds turn dark.
A sleety drift from mountaintops drags down the hills
And quivering gleams of light make trailheads
                Shimmer.
Now, in the turbulent, tumbling, tormenting weather,
As if the spirits know that spring is forthcoming,
A skylark sings a hopeful song.

THE COUGAR

I saw a cougar come ambling down the trail.
As graceful as a bit of cottonseed
That flits on breeze, he travelled on his way,
Intent on busy business of his own,
Secluded, as in a dream, in the realm
Of sights and sounds and scents and scores
That fill his day. Enclosed in my human world,
I watched the cougar with caution. Then suddenly,
His sauntering stride fractured; his velvet ears
Twitched;
His savvy instincts sought the air for clues;
He stepped towards the trail edge for shelter.
Cautious, I saw how thin the veil was -
Only a cliff edge, distant hilltop, and
The shadows of tall trees.

Then further down the trail they came: a hiking
Party of five, with bear-bells and chatter. When
Passed,
The silence of the forest resumed once again.
I paused, and waited while I watched. Larks called;
A chipmunk foraged. The shadows of the trees
Swayed back and forth beneath mountain-bred winds.
As last I ventured ahead, at last broke the reverie
To see where he had fared. To the distant sastruga.
There was no cougar. Only broken stems of grass,
Disturbed dreams and the shadow of a mystery.

MOONLIGHT LUST

We walk together all night long
Striding through a landscape
Gleaming as if made of new memories.
The moon's so bright an idea
So clean and bright and near -
The rush of lust and blazing love
In fragile eyes
That shows how alive we were
Under moonlight skies.

MOSHANNON MEMORIES

Beneath the hills of bleak and bare
Lay memories of sacred ground,
Where dreams of summer fill the air
When wanderlust travel comes around.

From to dawn to dusk hikers seek
The journeys of ancient old,
And stride from valley to peek.
Mountain memories to behold.

Wanderlust fools weave through trees
To keep warm and dry,
When rains arrives on breeze
And veils drop from sky.

And dreams come to stray,
Beneath the Appalachian sun
As, in the old Americana way,
The annual journeys are done.

SEATLE DRUNKARD

Rain and mist
And an old wall
Against whose rugged face
An aged drunkard
Leans his weary body.
Sinewy arms huddled.
Thoughts and full blown
Dreams recoil
And rise again
Against the drifting rain.
Mist ascends slowly
From the Pacific shoreline.
Wet shine the forming
Dreams timed and small.
And steadily
The raindrops fall.
May I in future years recall
Drifting mist pall
From some oceanic shore
And rain and Seattle
And of the drunkard against the wall.

HILLS OF HARRISON STATE PARK

The forest hills lean towards the Atlantic sky
All bound in sunlit haze,
And easily the red-tailed kites fly,
Like effortless dreams lost on high,
On quiet midsummer days.

We see wild vistas of every hue
Along the striding hilltop miles.
Distant mountains puncture the view
And, staining the distant blue,
Valleys promising daily trials.

Long, summer hikes of carefree ease,
So soon promise to cease.
Relaxing under sun-warmed sky,
We share these moments to ply
Memories of midsummer peace.

RUNNING SPACE

Running space.
Now, almost a moment missed,
Time in grace
Halts my fevered pace.
Space
To slow, to breathe,
To dream, renew,
Absorb, be.
Nature's space
Laden with healing silence.
In silence, space,
In space, silence.
Running space
As a gift
Free-given.
Dirtbaggers flee.

RISING MORTALITY

They said that Death
Came early that year -
They little knew
The tricks the Gods of Fate
Hold tight so dear,
Or what fading time would do -
Trust not in dreams
So scattered this year.

THE GREEN AGENDA

Look outwards, lost people,
The dream is breaking,
The journey is waking
This new bright day,
When none defame us,
No restriction tame us,
Nor actions shame us,
Bring on less dismay.

Wilds holds the promise,
Dark forest-lover!
Living's nearly over,
And though long the walk,
Vast vistas will greet us,
New kinship greet us,
And joy complete us
In the new wilderness talk.

So brood no more
On the journeys behind you,
The adventure before you,
Shall replace the past
When the green agenda
Cultivates the wise and stronger,
Holds back Man no longer
Before the vista vast.

THE OLD DRIFTER OF DAYTON

Who would begrudge the drifter old
His warm place by the fire,
His toke of consolation, and
His tales that never tire.
His place of honour at the edge.
His share in all good cheer,
Or any memories that help to make
His sojourn pleasant here?

MOOSHEHEAD LAKES

In the land of space and freedom,
Where a drifter can be alone,
Where deep forests climb the hills
And make the slopes their own.
From Bigelow to Aroostock,
There's memories made all the way,
And through each passing season
It allows the soul to stray.

THE SENIOR DIRTBAGGER

The ascent from the river
Was steep.
A very old dirtbagger,
Red-faced, determined,
Perched on a rock.
It gave me quite a shock
To see that he
Was lacing
Into his running shoes.

Surely, I thought,
He can't be going
Up there.
That is just where
I was wrong.
I saw him later
Far above my head
Half-way up the trail,
Resting, no doubt breathless,
On a ledge.
He'd made it so far.

Was he senile?
Was he brave?
Perhaps both, who knows.
But may the dirtbagger ever be
Running on trails
On ledges in the hills
And with all
Who, daring to run upwards,
Make it so far.

THE MARYLAND HILL

The golden rays of sun fall now upon
The land where once fires burned,
A hill now barren,
But looked upon once in a different light,
As just a harmonious and lonely place,
Where tortured souls all hope they hung,
The shaman, the stranger, and the like.

NEW YORK NELSON

I knew him but a little while,
That kind soul with a lasting smile.
He never rushed the journey bent,
And good deeds seemed his sole intent;
Not many knew his darkest plight
Whereby illness burnt blazing white,
Which meant that despite his prime of life
Darkness would prevail and seek strife,
And take his soul away.

But that was all some time gone by,
When Nelson's mind took sick and died,
So now I feel it's strange
That in my work I keep his name,
And through memories of time
His name and soul are set in rhyme.

THE TRAIL REFOUND

There is the path again,
The trail I lost
In the confusion,
In life's bitter pain,
Of toil unceasing
Battering stress and strain.

Wisely I see it now,
The trail, the way,
There, as it lay
Before my striding feet
On that other earlier day.

Yet this is not
The path I travelled before
But further up the coast.
Dirtbaggers abound be blessed.
Mist shroud, unwittingly,
I have at least lived
A little way progressed.

THE SLOW LOCOMOTIVE

The drunkard waited on the overpass
To freeze this moment,
Make it into memory.
And now that memory
Stirs us from the lost trail.
The vagabond, the drifter,
The wanderer,
All are gone.
Their tales, too, most likely.
The slow advancing locomotive
Of life and living
May yet survive
In someone's story.

WOODY

Walk softly past the black stately gates,
For here Guthrie sleeps,
Where he would most have wished,
Within the quiet solitude of Okfushee County,
The soft, familiar sounds of every day -
Traffic, birdsong, the tickle of wind through
Leaves -
Lulling his long dream with sheltered ease.

The kindly trees beyond Joplin Street
Sing befitting elegies.
One tiny stone on his resting place -
A small brass plaque set with gentle care
To mark his lifetime
On the journey in which he lies,
Among the Americana of memories.

FLEETING SOLITUDE MEMORIES

Fleeting is life whether dark or bright,
Time scatters memories among our flight.
For the fairest form and the widest eye.
Change as the weary years go by.
A brighter dream to my journey appears
Than all I have wished in wanderlust years;
I dream of solitude in perfect bliss.
When my soul is free from times like this.

THE SOLITARY DREAMER

I dream of landscapes with a gorgeous hue,
Under summer skies of azure blue,
Of majestic sunsets before the evening star,
Of vistas bright as diamonds by far,
Of journeys where drifters sing,
Of valleys were spirits are murmuring,
Of memories stronger than wealth and power,
Of solitary dreams my soul can devour,
Where promises and souls can change,
And visions can be bold and strange.
Americana landscapes soon shall seem,
Nothing more than a solitary dream.

SEEKING MORNING LIGHT

He feels the heartache
Taking hold tonight.
Only the wilderness trail
Can make it right.
Feeling the only,
Feeling lonely,
He needs the wild breeze
To hold him tight,
Hiking out till morning light.

THE MOUNTAIN RUNNERS

Each morning the little eager feet
Sprang up against the dawn breeze,
To plunge across the glowing stream
Up to the mountain trees;
And when the journey starts to test
They sought calm, far up the hills,
They bathed the windswept thirst
Among the mountain rills.

FOREST EDGE

'If you sit by the forest edge
At twilight and wait
Very quietly,
The coyotes will come,'
The Lakota mother had said.

So there we sat
Patiently, silently.
Springtime bugs danced
In the evening light.
Forest flies skated
Through the shadows
But no coyotes came.

We sat on unmoving.
We had almost forgotten
Why we were there.
And then
Suddenly, silently,
Stepping from nowhere
Into here,
The coyotes appeared,
Sniffing rapidly,
Nervously,
High and low,
To and fro.

MARYLAND FOREST

Sitting in the forest, taking in the air,
From the scent of pine, wafting everywhere,
Makes me count my blessings, whether rich or poor
To know the joy of travel who could ask for more.

Sitting in the forest, on a summer's day,
Listening to songbirds happily at play.
The echo of their calls carries through the trees,
What joy to travel on summer days like these.

Sitting in the forest after morning rain,
Watching all the treetops sway once again.
To hear the birds all singing surely this must be
A little bit of Americana for me to see.

Sitting in the forest at the end of day,
Knowing all the hours are fading fast away.
One must think of time when the journeys through
There will be the new trails, breaking fresh anew.

SUMMER SUNRISE

High within a mountain range of tall peeks,
Restless in a secluded glade I lie;
Dreams of Guthrie and Kerouac I fashion,
My vistas of drifting clouds and warming sky.

So still the forests that surround,
That scarce a shifting wind in the trees.
My thoughts and dreams slow to bake,
Though I'm chilled in mountain breeze;

These memories so vivid and clear
Wanderlust spirits within seek to float
To where the realms merge and weave
In journeys of sleepless remote.

THE WOODPECKER

In that cold hour
Before the dawn
Wins its diurnal battle
With the night
The woodpecker taps:
He feels the light
In my dark hour
Oh may there be
A wise sweet vision
Such as he.

LITTLE LOST VALLEY

There is a valley, shroud by the misty shire -
The mossy, Kentucky valley,
The little sanctuary where pines climb so high.
Among the hills aslant
The wanderlust chant;
Along lower slopes the drifters lie
In lazy camp smoke, more stoned, more still
Than the faint wood smoke of any cabin fire.
Here some calm sprites leads me by the hand
And all my heart is lifted by the hold,
Of promises made so bold
In smoke, and touch, and any hidden trail bend:
And out from every venture steals a friend.

WILDS WONDER

I take my first look at the mountains,
And blink my dazzled eyes -
When I see wonders touch the skies.
Standing at the trail's edge,
Momentarily taken aback -
Clutching at my hobo sack.

Still now I like to stand and stare -
Still taken breathless by beauty everywhere.
The magic and mystery,
Heart and soul feel the strain -
So worth the traveller's pain.

CALL OF THE WILD HILLS

Memories of the past are seeping,
Kerouac calling, in echoes of time,
Words of solitude, haunting,
From hills on the Americana vine.

In wildness, mountains stretch and rise
Whose majesty weave through minds,
Stories and tales from weathered hills
Of ancient wanderlust of poetic kinds.

Country tales of mystic yearning,
Still the rushing heart for a beat,
Dreams of solitude and wanderings,
Under the Americana feet.

WILDERNESS SANCTUARY

Seek the wilderness if you favour peace of mind,
Where the wilds soothe gently, quiet and kind.
Seek sanctuary in some cloistered glade,
Take a lover deep in woods for breathless shade.

Savour the calming effect of warm, carefree air,
For wilderness can soothe even the hardest care.
Walk by where shallow creek ebb and flow,
Skinny-dip where only wild fauna dare to go.

An unseen remedy is the least of many things,
To be found where the wild songbird sings.
The morning sunshine brings the calming air,
The wilderness sanctuary worth every prayer.

SUMMERTIME LOVE

I watched her wake in the early sun,
Wearing nothing but an old summer gown,
She smiled at my lusty stare,
With a pensive, but happy frown.

I saw her lay down in the summer glade,
With an open frock to her knees,
Lying dreamlike as a sprite,
Casting off wishes beneath the trees.

But best of all, this summer day,
As the sun began to rise,
I felt her curves pressed beside me,
With soft beauty in her eyes.

MOHAWK STATE FOREST

The forest is a sanctuary on this summer day,
Welcoming any wanderlust fool who may stray.
Beauty and mystery conspire once again,
The forest alive and whispering after rain.

Ancient trails that snake through pockets of ferns,
Little secrets to reveal with twists and turns.
Unspoiled and wild as nature had planned,
This lovely wilderness land.

Soothing with vistas in kindest ways,
The forest cools on weary summer days.
Yet this wanderlust fool wanders by,
Seeking promises out under open sky.

WAKING EARLY

Last night fades. Warm morning light seeps
Under the doors and windows, up my back.
Sunshine begins to wedge between the crack
In the bedroom curtains and the lover sways.
A single limb sweeps against the sheets,
A murmur the heart deceives.
Aches beat like storms appearing. I draw
The sheet across the distorted face I saw.
Find shelter. Late dreams bustle in the eaves.

LEXY

Lexy, I know I don't know you,
But I wish I could,
Despite the fact that
You'd probably think me crazy
But I promise I'd be good.
We could make it work,
Though I know it sounds hazy.
I know we'd make some magic.
We could be so right.
And though you don't know me
Can't we just run into the night?

SAN MIGUEL VALLEY

I wander underneath a summer sky,
Pierced by the lone eagle's cry.
Back home, by comfort from desert cabin
fire
Reluctant words found are drawn
While buzzard solo, wild and free
Watches from the spire of a tree…

From outer trail ways that I stroll
Came wild wanderlusts of the soul.

GHOST IN THE NIGHT

I sleep by the lost mountain stream,
Deep down in the darkness of dream.
All my life I kinda always knew,
The ghost of Dad I'd see come true,
Taking hold of my soul tight.

I live as a wild and lonesome soul,
Lost in dark dreams beyond control.
Even under distant mountain sleep
The wilds held drifting memories deep.

For the ghost holds my soul tight,
Deep in my dreams of night.
All my life I kinda always knew,
The ghost of Dad I'd see come true,
Taking hold of my soul tight.

VIRGINIA SUMMER

The distant mountains rise above ancient pines,
No secrets or revelation do they now hold.
The scarred giants grated by modern times,
The land fractured and old.

The sluggish trails meander under feet,
The forest ways left behind in lore.
The wanderlust fools dizzy in summer heat,
Amble carefree across the Virginia floor.

Yet magic spots, too sacred to name,
Still light the wilderness ways.
And hardy exploration flame
Burns for outdoor strays.

And though tarnished hills proudly stand
Raped to earth and bare,
The majesty of the American land
Hides majestic moments everywhere.

THE CAMP FIRE

When the rain of summer fell,
Drifters to the camp came,
Gathering round the fire to tell
Stories by the camp-fire flame.

Americana passed down of old,
Folk music, guitars play -
Tales to forget the nightly cold;
Stories that haunt the country day.

Some spoke of a moonshine crone
Tales of how he did fare;
Stories old and well-known,
In hills that became his lair.

Country folk in the forest den
Shared of journeys yet to be,
Others told of odd mountain men
Who had wandered in from sea.

Americana lore to spice the heart,
Drives out the rainy chill.
Storytelling - the dying art,
Brings me magic and smiles still.

NEW HAMPSHIRE SUMMER

In New Hampshire, when trails are divine,
How majestic is the summer scene:
Rolling hills to valleys fine
As well as secret glades of green.

Reflected on lakes expanding and still
Giant trees from larch to majestic oak.
Drifters and hikers converge every hill -
Wanderlust dreams needing to stoke.

Fluffy clouds flitting in summers skies,
Painting pictures of America pure.
Vistas of beauty for adventurous eyes,
Leaving the avid walker wanting more.

The warmth, the pure sunshine light,
Gleams on wild trails where folk do roam.
Down country tracks, on mountains might,
Holds the wanton heart seeking a home.

SUMMER DAYS ON SUMMER TRAILS

Long aisles of trails stretch away,
Mysterious with wanderlust ways;
And their journeys drifters play
A majesty, nights and days.

Across the hills the hikers sing,
Their shadows, stirred
Faintly, like eagles on wing,
And moans never heard.

Once more I join the summer trail,
Through solitude's country bold,
Unimagined vistas that never fail,
Till dusk shrinks and shadows fold.

THE LAST DAY OF JUNE

Where is that laughing Sprite so fair,
With lustrous eyes and flaming hair.
That walked the summer trail awhile,
Gladdening the journey with her wicked smile?
With tales that in her own cheeky way,
She shared on the summer day?
The journey stands open - June has sped
Over the memories with airy tred,
Scattering the emotions on our way,
Piling the emotions while we stray;
And playful words I loved the best
She borne away from her breast:
And from the wanderlust way
We shared the summer day
While I miss, today, her playful tune
She sang on the last day of June.

SAFE CORNER OF TOWN

Often I want to hide
In the safe corner of town
And lure myself to sleep
And cure myself of pain.
But deep down inside I know
I've got to follow the greats,
Great writers and poets, artists
And dreamers,
Earn my right to be living
In the safe corner of town
Memories there to keep,
Desires there to gain.

SUMMER IDEALS

Late brunch at the cabin door,
Dog relaxed upon the floor.
Starling, swift, dove and thrush
In the warm morning hush.
Songbirds chatter in the trees.
Drifters relax in summer breeze,
Soothed in the honeysuckle.
Down the trail hikers chuckle;
In the meadow mules bray;
Wanderlust fool seek to stray.
Morning mist lifts
Towards the sunshine drifts.
Optimism scents the morning air -
Summer months of beauty rare.

EARLY MAINE FALL

The journeys now are slowing down,
Man and Nature take a pause.
The woodlands change to golden brown,
The chilly nights till winter's cause.

Trade winds blow from Atlantic seas,
Hikers pack for turbulent trails.
The shades of reds in fallen leaves,
Journeys bring many fails.

Mountain peaks shroud in white,
Chilly winds all too soon.
The valleys hide, ghostly-bright
Under the glistening evening moon.

Silence now songbirds fly.
Nature hordes against the cold.
Campfires lit as sunny days die,
Wanderlust left for just the bold.

NORTH CAROLINA COAST

The cool morning mist lifts,
Sunshine stoically burns through,
And all along the Carolina coast
The summer day breaks out anew.

The azure blue of sea and sky
Providing a wanderlust canopy
For all the soft summer beauty
Beside the Carolina sea.

The rhythm of the transient,
The pleasant way of life,
Brings understanding and peace
And heals the urban strife.

SUNRISE FOR THE DEAD

Low light of sunrise now
Faintly over the sleeping valley.
Old drifter first to wake remembers:
First thing every dawn
Remember the wilds, cry for them.
Softly at first his tears begin,
One by one as we wake and hear
Join in the memory, and the whole valley
Cries for the wilds, the poor wilds
Gone from here to the Ghost Realm:
Solitude is remembered.
Then it is over, journey now,
Trails found, laughter now,
And a new trek calling.

THE TRAILS END

In wanderlust hours, we choose the trails,
We know not care or sorrow,
With joy and hope, we drift along
Unmindful of tomorrow.

But soon the journeys grow dim with tears,
The joy with sorrow blended,
And mist our paths enshroud,
Till life's wild dream is ended.

We sigh and weep by those who wait
The wait that knows no waking;
The town is blest, they are at rest,
The while our souls are aching.

At trails end they watch and wait,
They watch and wait our coming;
So fair and bright, in summer light,
While we wanderers feel the gloaming.

CAROLINA CHARM

From turbulent seas
To hilltop breeze,
I catch the dreams of few
And follow where eagle spirits flew.
While in the valleys of Jackson,
Trails climb and curl around,
Where once meandered huntsmen,
Now poet types abound.
They try to capture Carolina charm,
And they try to share, brothers band
With words and tales of lore
In that ancient Carolina land.

INVITATION TO RUN

Run with me now
In the dusky spring light.
Run with me now
Under the desert sky.
Run with all your might
And race me
And lead me
And follow me
And imagine you can fly.
Watch the changing land
And the colours of the trail
That seems so still
Run with me, friend,
Like you've lived all your life
Away from stress and strife
On the blessed hill.

A PORTRAIT OF TRAVEL

I tried to tell the story
Of how I really feel.
The trails took and stories told
To make it all seem real.
Not one journey was joy enough,
Each involved a certain pain.
Not one trail was hard enough,
To not make me travel again.
Not one person dark enough,
To make me want isolation.
In the end I had wandered,
Worn, frayed and almost broke,
But travel brings me so much more,
Footsteps and trails in lands of hope.

HOLLYWOOD BOUND

Oh, friend, let us travel far away.
Let us got to the American West,
To lands scorched in tales and trails,
To where vagabonds go to rest.
Let us swap stories with stars,
In coffee shops, beachside is best.
Let us get lost,
Where our dreams can tangle,
Our hearts and souls can stir.
Not least forget where we were.

CHILDHOOD DREAMS

I was raised on walking and sunshine
Barefoot in meadows and down dirt roads
I hide amongst the animals and trees
Making up my own stories and codes
Seeking out the local solitude
Leaving home at the crack of dawn
I enjoyed the wide-open spaces
With meadows replacing lawn;
I loved my countryside adventures
And walking conquered my foes
I was raised on walking and sunshine
And share the fact so everyone knows.

A WALK WITH AMERICANA

Dreamy, drastic, Americana days
Of summer sun and majestic vistas,
Of sweeping hills and winding valleys,
Of turquoise streams and crystal lakes,
And Americana - fused and famed.

The mountains, grand and snowy white,
Stretch out before, mile on mile,
While beat poems and fabled stories,
Dance dizzily from memory to memory
In endless, ageless tales of lore.

The joy sublime of Americana,
Who reveals in the simple things,
Like golden songs and lullabies,
And old tattoos, and faded paintings,
And mysteries that hold the test of time.

THE PRIDE AND PAIN OF TRAIL RUNNING

As we made our way towards the conclusion of the final stage of the race I was faced with a scene that was all too familiar: a blistering finish and a gap to close. I knew exactly what I had to do. As soon as I hit the flatter sections of the trail I was itching to get going. I ramped up the pace as the gradient pitched and plunged itself through the Californian landscape. I too plunged into a familiar zone of anguish and discomfort. I felt confident, my legs pushed hard, but my mind was relaxed. I felt alive, strong, and optimistic about getting to the end of the run. I found my pain threshold and I kept nudging at the edges of it to allow me to go that little bit extra, to go faster.

The battle in my mind began. It was one that I had played so many times before. I had to close that gap to the other runners. No matter how fast the elites were going I had to maintain the distance. It was a battle I fought blindly, always telling myself that they had plenty in their reserves, and demanded of myself that I find more of mine. With five miles to go the last check drew near: I knew the finish to be soon. I was keeping up, but not by enough. I had to push harder still. Whatever pace they were doing I had to match it.

With a little over two miles to go we shot out of the cliff tops and the Malibu beach loomed out ahead of us. I felt dwarfed by the enormity of the landscape: stunning beaches, coastal paths, ocean-side cities. I surveyed the stupendous world of cliffs and ocean, thinking: 'There is nowhere else I would rather be.'

The views were awe-inspiring: cliffs tumbling into foaming sea, spray lapping the trails. Every bend in the race had unveiled a scene more dramatic than the last.

I clawed back the distance between myself and the pack ahead like a man dragging himself towards safety. For the next few minutes I squeezed out everything, every ounce of energy and motivation I had. I timed my efforts like a professional. As we neared the final banner, it was practically done. I had made the cut and for the first time since starting I found myself on the heels of another runner.

I had been so focused on catching this lead group that when they loomed up ahead of me suddenly my mind went silent. I was flooded with emotions: elation, relief, tears. I had done what was needed. I had persisted and proved myself in my own eyes. There was no disappointment to fear of that day.

But I wasn't done. With only minutes to recover, and without a plan forming in my mind, pure drive took over. With two miles to go I dug deep and pushed.

I was running really well, steady and yet aggressive, the perfect combination. The pain is a constant background now: my body was searching for oxygen, mouth is open, throat being rasped by the rush of sea air. Messages of strain and stress were put aside for the time being, my brain is stoic - keep it up, this is good, deal with it.

The gap between myself and the lead group closed up a little. I looked over my shoulder once and those behind were straggling and already looked smaller; I looked over a second time and they seemed to have disappeared. As I looked forward I saw the finishing line. A feeling came over me that had been so suppressed that I thought I had learnt to deny its existence. I felt that rushing-joy that I was going to make the finish.

There was just metres between that finish line and my feet. I could see the flags that lined the final twist and turn towards that line. I was so close. My heart had been bursting out of my chest. Now it seemed to bury itself into a cheesy grin. At that moment, as I beamed a smile and the tears mixed into the sweat and dirt of the dusty trails that covered my face, I knew the truth about trail running: it's bloody worth all the effort.

MATT HAYDEN

WAKING UP IN NEW MEXICO

I had been dreaming about this experience for some time. The landscape at the edge of town was a country barren and sun-baked, with canyons and wind-sculpted sandstone hills. It appealed to my vagabond imagination.

Inhospitable. Desolate. Savage. All terms that I had found when picking up a guide book about New Mexico. Apart from a few lonely homesteads, this is epic country - a bewitching place.

'It's like being at the edge of the world, isn't it?' I said to my friend, who just nodded absent-mindedly in replay, his thoughts occupied by a piece of white sun-dried animal skull he held in his hands.

Although not *actually* at the edge of the world, the quiet town in New Mexico, whose trails I was exploring by bike, feels pretty wild.

Wildness is seductive to my friend and I insomuch as it always manages to give us a way to touch on a natural world much grander than ourselves; an opportunity to reflect on our state of being and our place within the world, and to experience a remoteness, isolation or strangeness that's like a sting in the comfort of everyday life. For a place to feel rewardingly wild for me, it needs to fire up parts of my soul equally solitary and primitive. New Mexico certainly does that.

The weather had been cool and calm when we set off, but it wasn't long before the harsh, blighting desert conditions kicked in. Dust storms and intense humidity accompanied increasingly challenging terrain: steep hillsides, dried riverbeds and cracked trails. Biking and walking our way across this wild landscape, we finally arrived at our digs just before suppertime.

The brick cabin we were staying in was clean and spacious, if a little spartan and derelict. But it was soon improved infinitely by my friend putting on some fresh coffee and preparing a meal of beans and rice. Our aching limbs soothed by food and chat, we decided to sit in blissful contentment outdoors by a campfire and watch the evening sky slowly expand into a vastness of stars and planets. We were both fairly quiet and thoughtful as it finally sunk in that after months of planning this trip we were on the trail.

The next morning, after plenty of strong coffee and home-made flapjacks, we were ready to another day's biking. It wasn't long before the nagging anxiety of being out in the wildness was being replaced with a growing confidence in our trail-riding skills. So far on the trip neither of us had admitted defeat on any of the trails we had ridden. We felt all but unstoppable.

That was until day three. The plan had been to navigate the ridge of some nearby mountains, but a heat wave had made the going so difficult, even my local-born friend deemed it unwise. Instead, he led the way to a small town, where we spent the rest of the day sipping coffee and eating pancakes in the diner and pausing to admire the surroundings outside the windows: an arresting sprawl of reds and browns offset by the muted greens of distant hills.

Though the last day had been a blunt reminder that we don't always triumph over nature, I could still tell the New Mexico wilds had worked its magic. My friend and I are happier versions of ourselves who stepped out just a few days ago; soothed by the grandeur, awed by the views and buoyed by the wild spaces of one of America's wildest lands.

MATT HAYDEN

WALKING WITHIN TREES

The sea started to swell as we left the Oregon harbour. The waves grew frisky, tossing the small fishing boat about as if it were a little-ducky in a bath. Fortunately, I'm a stoic sailor. My instincts to grab a life vest and yell: 'Save yourselves!' rattled in the forefront of my mind. I sat, watching white-capped waves rise and fall, and tried not to throw up on my friend, Cathy Lightfoot Hayes, a beautiful First Nations guide and boat owner, I'd happily accepted spending a day with. Then suddenly, in the lee of cedar-treed cliffs, we pulled into a small port. Everything calmed. 'We survived!' I cried to Cathy, who had already disembarked to moor us to the wooden jetty. I followed, dropped briefly to my knees to kiss the salty wooden boards of the quay, and we walked off towards the woods.

This was an ambiguous start to the day. I had travelled to the north coast of Oregon for some adventure. Nothing too grand. I have left it a little late to be the first man to cycle the moon. I find walking around the local millpond enjoyment enough on a given day. I am easily contented. When I talk of adventure, I mean a woodland walk, with hopefully a coffee shop nearby.

So I made for northwest American and its string of small forested islands, on the premise that islands are wild - because of the obvious accessibility problems - but only slightly so. There are plenty to visit. All are essentially wild and solitary. Some are thankfully undeveloped, as the Pacific Northwest was before tourism got a hold. It's a relatively unspoilt paradise where discerning travellers can find natural sanctuary among the rugged wooded islands, and where pristine landscape and First Nations heritage dance their unique tango.

Without a doubt, as I followed Cathy from the quay, I felt I was in the company of a very special friend. Travel is just a great bonder. Cathy is a super-friendly woman with an impressive head of jet black hair and both arms solid with flowered-tattoos. Her heritage is Tsimshian First Nation, but her thinking is nothing but forward.

Listening to Cathy talk about the coastline, the tales of fishermen, bears and loggers, it's clear she loves her job as a guide. It's like watching a peace-envoy at work: bringing people together by sharing the love of the outdoors.

Cathy and I had become friends on a social-media website, and had shared a common interest in - Shinrin Yoku - the Japanese art of 'Forest Bathing'. Of course, it doesn't involving lugging bathtubs into woodlands or actually immersing yourself into water, but simply being enclosed in woodlands and enjoying the sensory bombardment of the natural world. Researchers at Japan's Chiba University had recorded that spending time in forests can lower stress hormones as well as pulse rate and blood pressure. It was subject that Cathy and I both fascinating. Visiting Oregon was now giving us the opportunity to share the experience.

We carried on up through the outlying edges of the forest. As many as nine bald eagles were wheeling overhead and searching from the skies, as they peered down for prey.

The forest edge loomed up ahead. A small trailhead marked the way. I felt a tinge of wonder and excitement. It seemed a faintly ominous place that to me at least, made me feel wary with a potent ional that's hard to rationalise. Getting lost, making discoveries, exploring Huckleberry Finn-style, encounters with wild creatures and getting that magical reminder of what adventures can be had with travels and friendships.

And in between the trees we walked.

MATT HAYDEN

Printed in Great Britain
by Amazon